50 German Pancake and Waffle Recipes

By: Kelly Johnson

Table of Contents

- Classic German Pancake
- Apple Cinnamon German Pancakes
- Lemon Ricotta German Pancakes
- Nutella-Stuffed German Pancakes
- Blueberry German Pancakes
- Raspberry German Pancakes with Powdered Sugar
- Banana Foster German Pancakes
- German Pancakes with Sausage and Maple Syrup
- Savory German Pancakes with Spinach and Cheese
- Chocolate Chip German Pancakes
- Peach German Pancakes
- Pear and Almond German Pancakes
- German Pancakes with Streusel Topping
- Caramelized Onion and Bacon German Pancakes
- Pumpkin Spice German Pancakes
- Strawberry German Pancakes with Whipped Cream
- Pineapple German Pancakes with Coconut

- Cinnamon Roll German Pancakes
- Cherry German Pancakes
- German Pancakes with Lemon Curd
- Zesty Orange German Pancakes
- Maple Bacon German Pancakes
- S'mores German Pancakes
- Coconut Cream German Pancakes
- Mocha German Pancakes
- Waffle Cone German Pancakes
- Tropical Fruit German Pancakes
- Sweet Potato German Pancakes
- Bacon and Cheese Waffle Pancakes
- Belgian Waffle Pancakes with Strawberries
- Nutty Banana Waffle Pancakes
- Cinnamon Roll Waffle Pancakes
- Maple Pecan Waffle Pancakes
- Raspberry Cream Cheese Waffle Pancakes
- Chocolate Hazelnut Waffle Pancakes
- Waffle Pancakes with Blueberry Compote

- Almond Butter Waffle Pancakes
- Pumpkin Waffle Pancakes
- Lemon Poppy Seed Waffle Pancakes
- Cranberry Orange Waffle Pancakes
- Waffle Pancakes with Fresh Mango Salsa
- Almond Joy Waffle Pancakes
- Sweet and Salty Waffle Pancakes with Pretzels
- Mocha Chip Waffle Pancakes
- Caramel Waffle Pancakes with Pecans
- Churro Waffle Pancakes
- Waffle Pancakes with Peanut Butter and Jelly
- Cherry Cheesecake Waffle Pancakes
- Dark Chocolate Raspberry Waffle Pancakes
- Cinnamon Apple Waffle Pancakes

Classic German Pancake
Ingredients:

- 1 cup all-purpose flour
- 1 cup milk
- 4 large eggs
- 1/4 cup unsalted butter (melted)
- 1/4 tsp salt
- 1 tsp vanilla extract
- Powdered sugar (for dusting)
- Lemon wedges (optional, for serving)

Instructions:
Preheat your oven to 425°F (220°C).
In a blender, combine the flour, milk, eggs, melted butter, salt, and vanilla extract. Blend until smooth.
Pour the batter into a greased 9x13-inch baking dish or a cast-iron skillet.
Bake for 20-25 minutes, or until the pancake puffs up and turns golden brown.
Remove from the oven and immediately dust with powdered sugar.
Serve with lemon wedges for a traditional touch, or your favorite syrup.

Apple Cinnamon German Pancakes

Ingredients:

- 1 cup all-purpose flour
- 1 cup milk
- 4 large eggs
- 1/4 cup unsalted butter (melted)
- 1/4 tsp salt
- 1 tsp vanilla extract
- 1 tsp ground cinnamon
- 2 apples (peeled, cored, and sliced)
- 2 tbsp brown sugar
- Powdered sugar (for dusting)

Instructions:

Preheat your oven to 425°F (220°C).

In a blender, combine the flour, milk, eggs, melted butter, salt, vanilla extract, and ground cinnamon. Blend until smooth.

In a skillet over medium heat, melt 1 tbsp of butter and sauté the apple slices with the brown sugar and cinnamon until the apples are tender (about 5 minutes). Set aside.

Pour the batter into a greased 9x13-inch baking dish or a cast-iron skillet.

Add the cooked apples on top of the batter, spreading them evenly.

Bake for 20-25 minutes, or until the pancake puffs up and turns golden brown.

Dust with powdered sugar before serving.

Lemon Ricotta German Pancakes
Ingredients:

- 1 cup all-purpose flour
- 1 cup milk
- 4 large eggs
- 1/4 cup unsalted butter (melted)
- 1/4 tsp salt
- 1 tsp vanilla extract
- 1/2 cup ricotta cheese
- Zest of 1 lemon
- 2 tbsp fresh lemon juice
- Powdered sugar (for dusting)
- Fresh berries (optional, for serving)

Instructions:
Preheat your oven to 425°F (220°C).
In a blender, combine the flour, milk, eggs, melted butter, salt, vanilla extract, ricotta cheese, lemon zest, and lemon juice. Blend until smooth.
Pour the batter into a greased 9x13-inch baking dish or a cast-iron skillet.
Bake for 20-25 minutes, or until the pancake puffs up and turns golden brown.
Dust with powdered sugar and serve with fresh berries if desired.

Nutella-Stuffed German Pancakes

Ingredients:

- 1 cup all-purpose flour
- 1 cup milk
- 4 large eggs
- 1/4 cup unsalted butter (melted)
- 1/4 tsp salt
- 1 tsp vanilla extract
- 1/2 cup Nutella
- Powdered sugar (for dusting)
- Fresh strawberries or bananas (optional, for serving)

Instructions:

Preheat your oven to 425°F (220°C).
In a blender, combine the flour, milk, eggs, melted butter, salt, and vanilla extract. Blend until smooth.
Pour the batter into a greased 9x13-inch baking dish or a cast-iron skillet.
Add spoonfuls of Nutella on top of the batter, spreading it in a few places across the pancake.
Bake for 20-25 minutes, or until the pancake puffs up and turns golden brown.
Dust with powdered sugar and serve with fresh strawberries or bananas, if desired.

Blueberry German Pancakes
 Ingredients:

- 1 cup all-purpose flour
- 1 cup milk
- 4 large eggs
- 1/4 cup unsalted butter (melted)
- 1/4 tsp salt
- 1 tsp vanilla extract
- 1 cup fresh blueberries
- Powdered sugar (for dusting)

Instructions:
Preheat your oven to 425°F (220°C).
In a blender, combine the flour, milk, eggs, melted butter, salt, and vanilla extract. Blend until smooth.
Pour the batter into a greased 9x13-inch baking dish or a cast-iron skillet.
Sprinkle the fresh blueberries on top of the batter.
Bake for 20-25 minutes, or until the pancake puffs up and turns golden brown.
Dust with powdered sugar before serving.

Raspberry German Pancakes with Powdered Sugar
Ingredients:

- 1 cup all-purpose flour
- 1 cup milk
- 4 large eggs
- 1/4 cup unsalted butter (melted)
- 1/4 tsp salt
- 1 tsp vanilla extract
- 1 cup fresh raspberries
- Powdered sugar (for dusting)

Instructions:
Preheat your oven to 425°F (220°C).
In a blender, combine the flour, milk, eggs, melted butter, salt, and vanilla extract. Blend until smooth.
Pour the batter into a greased 9x13-inch baking dish or a cast-iron skillet.
Scatter the fresh raspberries over the top of the batter.
Bake for 20-25 minutes, or until the pancake puffs up and turns golden brown.
Dust with powdered sugar before serving.

Banana Foster German Pancakes
Ingredients:

- 1 cup all-purpose flour
- 1 cup milk
- 4 large eggs
- 1/4 cup unsalted butter (melted)
- 1/4 tsp salt
- 1 tsp vanilla extract
- 2 ripe bananas (sliced)
- 1/4 cup dark rum
- 2 tbsp brown sugar
- 1/2 tsp ground cinnamon
- Powdered sugar (for dusting)

Instructions:
Preheat your oven to 425°F (220°C).
In a blender, combine the flour, milk, eggs, melted butter, salt, and vanilla extract. Blend until smooth.
Pour the batter into a greased 9x13-inch baking dish or a cast-iron skillet.
In a skillet, melt 1 tbsp of butter over medium heat. Add the banana slices, brown sugar, and cinnamon. Stir gently for a couple of minutes until the bananas are softened.
Add the dark rum to the skillet (be careful when adding the rum), and cook for another 1-2 minutes.
Top the baked pancake with the banana foster mixture.
Dust with powdered sugar before serving.

German Pancakes with Sausage and Maple Syrup
Ingredients:

- 1 cup all-purpose flour
- 1 cup milk
- 4 large eggs
- 1/4 cup unsalted butter (melted)
- 1/4 tsp salt
- 1 tsp vanilla extract
- 4 cooked breakfast sausage links (sliced)
- Maple syrup (for serving)

Instructions:
Preheat your oven to 425°F (220°C).
In a blender, combine the flour, milk, eggs, melted butter, salt, and vanilla extract. Blend until smooth.
Pour the batter into a greased 9x13-inch baking dish or a cast-iron skillet.
Scatter the sliced sausage pieces over the batter.
Bake for 20-25 minutes, or until the pancake puffs up and turns golden brown.
Serve with warm maple syrup.

Savory German Pancakes with Spinach and Cheese
 Ingredients:

- 1 cup all-purpose flour
- 1 cup milk
- 4 large eggs
- 1/4 cup unsalted butter (melted)
- 1/4 tsp salt
- 1 tsp garlic powder
- 1 cup fresh spinach (chopped)
- 1 cup shredded cheese (cheddar, mozzarella, or a mix)

Instructions:
Preheat your oven to 425°F (220°C).
In a blender, combine the flour, milk, eggs, melted butter, salt, and garlic powder. Blend until smooth.
Pour the batter into a greased 9x13-inch baking dish or a cast-iron skillet.
Sprinkle the chopped spinach and shredded cheese evenly over the batter.
Bake for 20-25 minutes, or until the pancake puffs up and turns golden brown.
Serve immediately for a savory meal.

Chocolate Chip German Pancakes

Ingredients:

- 1 cup all-purpose flour
- 1 cup milk
- 4 large eggs
- 1/4 cup unsalted butter (melted)
- 1/4 tsp salt
- 1 tsp vanilla extract
- 1/2 cup mini chocolate chips
- Powdered sugar (for dusting)

Instructions:

Preheat your oven to 425°F (220°C).
In a blender, combine the flour, milk, eggs, melted butter, salt, and vanilla extract. Blend until smooth.
Pour the batter into a greased 9x13-inch baking dish or a cast-iron skillet.
Sprinkle the mini chocolate chips evenly on top of the batter.
Bake for 20-25 minutes, or until the pancake puffs up and turns golden brown.
Dust with powdered sugar before serving.

Peach German Pancakes
Ingredients:

- 1 cup all-purpose flour
- 1 cup milk
- 4 large eggs
- 1/4 cup unsalted butter (melted)
- 1/4 tsp salt
- 1 tsp vanilla extract
- 2 peaches (peeled, pitted, and sliced)
- Powdered sugar (for dusting)

Instructions:
Preheat your oven to 425°F (220°C).
In a blender, combine the flour, milk, eggs, melted butter, salt, and vanilla extract. Blend until smooth.
Pour the batter into a greased 9x13-inch baking dish or a cast-iron skillet.
Scatter the sliced peaches on top of the batter.
Bake for 20-25 minutes, or until the pancake puffs up and turns golden brown.
Dust with powdered sugar before serving.

Pear and Almond German Pancakes

Ingredients:

- 1 cup all-purpose flour
- 1 cup milk
- 4 large eggs
- 1/4 cup unsalted butter (melted)
- 1/4 tsp salt
- 1 tsp vanilla extract
- 2 pears (peeled, cored, and sliced)
- 1/4 cup sliced almonds
- Powdered sugar (for dusting)

Instructions:

Preheat your oven to 425°F (220°C).
In a blender, combine the flour, milk, eggs, melted butter, salt, and vanilla extract. Blend until smooth.
Pour the batter into a greased 9x13-inch baking dish or a cast-iron skillet.
Top the batter with the sliced pears and sliced almonds.
Bake for 20-25 minutes, or until the pancake puffs up and turns golden brown.
Dust with powdered sugar before serving.

German Pancakes with Streusel Topping
Ingredients:
For the pancake:

- 1 cup all-purpose flour
- 1 cup milk
- 4 large eggs
- 1/4 cup unsalted butter (melted)
- 1/4 tsp salt
- 1 tsp vanilla extract

For the streusel:

- 1/3 cup brown sugar
- 1/4 cup all-purpose flour
- 1/2 tsp cinnamon
- 3 tbsp cold butter (cut into cubes)

Instructions:
Preheat your oven to 425°F (220°C).
Blend the pancake ingredients until smooth. Pour the batter into a greased 9x13-inch baking dish or cast-iron skillet.
In a small bowl, mix the streusel ingredients with your fingers or a fork until crumbly. Sprinkle the streusel over the batter.
Bake for 20–25 minutes until puffed and golden. Let cool slightly, then serve warm.

Caramelized Onion and Bacon German Pancakes
Ingredients:

- 1 cup all-purpose flour
- 1 cup milk
- 4 large eggs
- 1/4 cup unsalted butter (melted)
- 1/4 tsp salt
- 1 tsp thyme (optional)
- 1 cup caramelized onions
- 1/2 cup cooked, crumbled bacon

Instructions:
Preheat your oven to 425°F (220°C).
Sauté onions slowly in butter until caramelized (20–25 minutes). Cook and crumble the bacon.
Blend the pancake ingredients until smooth. Pour the batter into a greased baking dish or skillet.
Top with caramelized onions and bacon.
Bake until golden and puffed, about 20–25 minutes. Serve warm.

Pumpkin Spice German Pancakes
 Ingredients:

- 3/4 cup all-purpose flour
- 3/4 cup milk
- 4 large eggs
- 1/4 cup pumpkin puree
- 1/4 cup unsalted butter (melted)
- 1/4 tsp salt
- 1 tsp vanilla extract
- 1 tsp pumpkin pie spice
- Powdered sugar or maple syrup for serving

Instructions:
Preheat your oven to 425°F (220°C).
Blend all ingredients until smooth. Pour into a greased baking dish or skillet.
Bake for 20–25 minutes until puffed and golden.
Top with powdered sugar or warm maple syrup.

Strawberry German Pancakes with Whipped Cream
Ingredients:

- 1 cup all-purpose flour
- 1 cup milk
- 4 large eggs
- 1/4 cup unsalted butter (melted)
- 1/4 tsp salt
- 1 tsp vanilla extract
- 1 cup fresh strawberries (sliced)
- Whipped cream (for serving)

Instructions:
Preheat your oven to 425°F (220°C).
Blend the pancake batter ingredients until smooth. Pour into a greased baking dish or skillet.
Bake until golden and puffed.
Top with fresh strawberries and dollops of whipped cream before serving.

Pineapple German Pancakes with Coconut
Ingredients:

- 1 cup all-purpose flour
- 1 cup coconut milk or regular milk
- 4 large eggs
- 1/4 cup unsalted butter (melted)
- 1/4 tsp salt
- 1 tsp vanilla extract
- 1 cup chopped pineapple (fresh or drained canned)
- 1/4 cup shredded coconut (toasted if preferred)

Instructions:
Preheat your oven to 425°F (220°C).
Blend batter ingredients until smooth. Pour into a greased dish or skillet.
Add pineapple and coconut evenly across the top.
Bake until puffed and golden. Serve warm, optionally with a drizzle of honey.

Cinnamon Roll German Pancakes

Ingredients:

For the pancake:

- 1 cup all-purpose flour
- 1 cup milk
- 4 large eggs
- 1/4 cup unsalted butter (melted)
- 1/4 tsp salt
- 1 tsp vanilla extract

For the cinnamon swirl:

- 1/4 cup brown sugar
- 2 tbsp melted butter
- 1 tsp cinnamon

For the glaze:

- 1/2 cup powdered sugar
- 1 tbsp milk
- 1/4 tsp vanilla extract

Instructions:

Preheat your oven to 425°F (220°C).
Blend the pancake batter and pour into a greased pan.
Whisk the swirl ingredients and drizzle over the batter in a spiral.

Bake until golden and puffed, 20–25 minutes.
Mix glaze ingredients and drizzle over the warm pancake before serving.

Cherry German Pancakes
Ingredients:

- 1 cup all-purpose flour
- 1 cup milk
- 4 large eggs
- 1/4 cup unsalted butter (melted)
- 1/4 tsp salt
- 1 tsp almond extract or vanilla
- 1 cup pitted cherries (fresh or frozen and thawed)
- Powdered sugar (for dusting)

Instructions:
Preheat your oven to 425°F (220°C).
Blend batter ingredients. Pour into a greased dish.
Scatter cherries evenly over the top.
Bake for 20–25 minutes until puffed.
Dust with powdered sugar before serving.

German Pancakes with Lemon Curd

Ingredients:

- 1 cup all-purpose flour
- 1 cup milk
- 4 large eggs
- 1/4 cup unsalted butter (melted)
- 1/4 tsp salt
- 1 tsp vanilla extract
- Lemon curd (store-bought or homemade)
- Powdered sugar (for dusting)

Instructions:

Preheat your oven to 425°F (220°C).
Blend pancake batter until smooth and pour into a greased pan.
Bake until golden and puffed, 20–25 minutes.
Serve warm with spoonfuls of lemon curd and a dusting of powdered sugar.

Zesty Orange German Pancakes
Ingredients:

- 1 cup all-purpose flour
- 1 cup milk
- 4 large eggs
- 1/4 cup orange juice
- Zest of 1 orange
- 1/4 cup unsalted butter (melted)
- 1/4 tsp salt
- 2 tbsp sugar

Instructions:
Preheat oven to 425°F (220°C).
Blend all ingredients until smooth. Pour into a greased baking dish or skillet.
Bake for 20–25 minutes until puffed and golden.
Top with more orange zest and a dusting of powdered sugar if desired.

Maple Bacon German Pancakes
 Ingredients:

- 1 cup all-purpose flour
- 1 cup milk
- 4 large eggs
- 1/4 cup unsalted butter (melted)
- 1/4 tsp salt
- 1 tsp vanilla extract
- 5 strips of crispy bacon (crumbled)
- Maple syrup (for serving)

Instructions:
Preheat oven to 425°F (220°C).
Blend the batter ingredients. Pour into a greased dish.
Sprinkle crumbled bacon evenly over the batter.
Bake for 20–25 minutes. Serve with warm maple syrup.

S'mores German Pancakes
 Ingredients:

- 1 cup all-purpose flour
- 1 cup milk
- 4 large eggs
- 1/4 cup unsalted butter (melted)
- 1/4 tsp salt
- 1 tsp vanilla extract
- 1/2 cup mini marshmallows
- 1/2 cup chocolate chips
- 1/4 cup crushed graham crackers

Instructions:
Preheat oven to 425°F (220°C).
Blend the batter and pour into a greased dish.
Sprinkle marshmallows, chocolate chips, and graham crackers evenly over the batter.
Bake for 20–25 minutes. Serve warm.

Coconut Cream German Pancakes

Ingredients:

- 1 cup all-purpose flour
- 1 cup coconut milk
- 4 large eggs
- 1/4 cup melted coconut oil or butter
- 1/4 tsp salt
- 1 tsp vanilla extract
- 1/4 cup sweetened shredded coconut
- Whipped coconut cream (for topping)

Instructions:

Preheat oven to 425°F (220°C).
Blend all ingredients and pour into a greased dish.
Bake for 20–25 minutes.
Top with whipped coconut cream and extra coconut shreds.

Mocha German Pancakes

Ingredients:

- 1 cup all-purpose flour
- 3/4 cup milk
- 1/4 cup strong brewed coffee (cooled)
- 4 large eggs
- 1/4 cup melted butter
- 2 tbsp cocoa powder
- 1/4 tsp salt
- 2 tbsp sugar
- Chocolate shavings (optional topping)

Instructions:
Preheat oven to 425°F (220°C).
Blend all ingredients until smooth and pour into a greased dish.
Bake until puffed and set, about 20–25 minutes.
Top with chocolate shavings or whipped cream.

Waffle Cone German Pancakes
Ingredients:

- 1 cup all-purpose flour
- 1 cup milk
- 4 large eggs
- 1/4 cup unsalted butter (melted)
- 1/4 tsp salt
- 1 tsp vanilla extract
- 1/4 cup crushed waffle cones
- Mini chocolate chips (optional)

Instructions:
Preheat oven to 425°F (220°C).
Blend batter ingredients and pour into a greased pan.
Sprinkle crushed waffle cone pieces (and chocolate chips, if using) over the batter.
Bake 20–25 minutes until golden and puffed.

Tropical Fruit German Pancakes
Ingredients:

- 1 cup all-purpose flour
- 1 cup coconut milk or regular milk
- 4 large eggs
- 1/4 cup butter (melted)
- 1/4 tsp salt
- 1 tsp vanilla extract
- 1/2 cup diced mango
- 1/2 cup diced pineapple
- 1/4 cup shredded coconut

Instructions:
Preheat oven to 425°F (220°C).
Blend the batter and pour into a greased pan.
Scatter the tropical fruits and coconut evenly.
Bake 20–25 minutes. Serve with a drizzle of honey or lime zest.

Sweet Potato German Pancakes

Ingredients:

- 3/4 cup mashed cooked sweet potato
- 3/4 cup all-purpose flour
- 3/4 cup milk
- 4 large eggs
- 1/4 cup melted butter
- 1/4 tsp salt
- 1 tsp cinnamon
- 1/2 tsp nutmeg
- 2 tbsp brown sugar

Instructions:

Preheat oven to 425°F (220°C).
Blend all ingredients until smooth. Pour into a greased baking dish.
Bake 20–25 minutes until golden and puffed.
Serve with maple syrup or a dollop of spiced whipped cream.

Bacon and Cheese Waffle Pancakes
Ingredients:

- 1 cup all-purpose flour
- 1 tsp baking powder
- 1/4 tsp salt
- 3/4 cup milk
- 1 egg
- 2 tbsp melted butter
- 1/2 cup shredded cheddar cheese
- 4 strips cooked bacon, crumbled

Instructions:
Mix dry ingredients. In a separate bowl, combine milk, egg, and melted butter.
Stir wet into dry, then fold in cheese and bacon.
Cook in waffle iron until golden and crispy.
Serve with maple syrup or hot sauce.

Belgian Waffle Pancakes with Strawberries

Ingredients:

- 1 cup all-purpose flour
- 1 tbsp sugar
- 1 tsp baking powder
- 1/4 tsp salt
- 3/4 cup buttermilk
- 1 egg
- 2 tbsp melted butter
- 1/2 tsp vanilla
- Fresh strawberries (sliced)
- Whipped cream (for topping)

Instructions:
Prepare batter and cook in waffle iron until golden and fluffy.
Top with fresh strawberries and whipped cream.

Nutty Banana Waffle Pancakes

Ingredients:

- 1 cup all-purpose flour
- 1 tbsp sugar
- 1 tsp baking powder
- 1/4 tsp salt
- 1 ripe banana (mashed)
- 3/4 cup milk
- 1 egg
- 2 tbsp melted butter
- 1/4 cup chopped walnuts or pecans

Instructions:
Mix dry ingredients. Combine banana, milk, egg, and butter.
Stir into dry mixture, then fold in nuts.
Cook in waffle iron. Serve with banana slices and maple syrup.

Cinnamon Roll Waffle Pancakes
 Ingredients:

- 1 cup all-purpose flour
- 1 tbsp sugar
- 1 tsp baking powder
- 1/2 tsp cinnamon
- 1/4 tsp salt
- 3/4 cup milk
- 1 egg
- 2 tbsp melted butter

Cream Cheese Glaze:

- 2 tbsp cream cheese
- 2 tbsp powdered sugar
- 1 tbsp milk
- 1/4 tsp vanilla

Instructions:
Prepare batter and cook in waffle iron.
Whisk glaze ingredients until smooth.
Drizzle glaze over warm waffles.

Maple Pecan Waffle Pancakes
Ingredients:

- 1 cup all-purpose flour
- 1 tbsp brown sugar
- 1 tsp baking powder
- 1/4 tsp salt
- 3/4 cup milk
- 1 egg
- 2 tbsp melted butter
- 1/4 cup chopped pecans
- Maple syrup (for serving)

Instructions:
Make batter, fold in pecans.
Cook in waffle iron. Serve with warm maple syrup and extra pecans.

Raspberry Cream Cheese Waffle Pancakes
Ingredients:

- 1 cup all-purpose flour
- 1 tbsp sugar
- 1 tsp baking powder
- 1/4 tsp salt
- 3/4 cup milk
- 1 egg
- 2 tbsp melted butter
- 1/4 cup fresh or frozen raspberries
- 2 tbsp cream cheese (cubed or swirled in)

Instructions:
Mix batter and gently fold in raspberries and cream cheese.
Cook in waffle iron.
Top with more raspberries and a sprinkle of powdered sugar.

Chocolate Hazelnut Waffle Pancakes
Ingredients:

- 1 cup all-purpose flour
- 2 tbsp sugar
- 1 tbsp cocoa powder
- 1 tsp baking powder
- 1/4 tsp salt
- 3/4 cup milk
- 1 egg
- 2 tbsp melted butter
- 1/4 cup chocolate chips or chopped hazelnuts
- Chocolate hazelnut spread (for topping)

Instructions:
Mix dry and wet ingredients. Fold in chips/nuts.
Cook in waffle iron.
Serve with a spread of chocolate hazelnut cream.

Waffle Pancakes with Blueberry Compote

Ingredients:

- 1 cup all-purpose flour
- 1 tbsp sugar
- 1 tsp baking powder
- 1/4 tsp salt
- 3/4 cup milk
- 1 egg
- 2 tbsp melted butter

Blueberry Compote:

- 1 cup blueberries
- 2 tbsp sugar
- 1 tbsp lemon juice
- 1 tsp cornstarch (optional for thickening)

Instructions:
Make the compote: simmer blueberries, sugar, and lemon juice until thickened.
Mix and cook waffle pancakes.
Top with warm blueberry compote.

Almond Butter Waffle Pancakes

Ingredients:

- 1 cup all-purpose flour
- 1 tbsp sugar
- 1 tsp baking powder
- 1/2 tsp baking soda
- 1/4 tsp salt
- 1 cup buttermilk
- 1 egg
- 1/4 cup almond butter
- 2 tbsp melted butter or oil
- 1/2 tsp vanilla extract

Instructions:
Whisk dry ingredients in one bowl. In another, mix wet ingredients, including almond butter.
Combine both mixtures just until smooth.
Pour into a preheated waffle iron and cook until golden.
Serve with honey or a drizzle of warm almond butter.

Pumpkin Waffle Pancakes
Ingredients:

- 1 cup all-purpose flour
- 2 tbsp brown sugar
- 1 tsp baking powder
- 1/2 tsp baking soda
- 1 tsp pumpkin pie spice
- 1/4 tsp salt
- 3/4 cup milk
- 1/2 cup pumpkin puree
- 1 egg
- 2 tbsp melted butter
- 1/2 tsp vanilla extract

Instructions:
Mix dry ingredients. In a separate bowl, whisk wet ingredients including pumpkin puree. Combine and cook in a waffle iron until crispy.
Top with whipped cream and maple syrup.

Lemon Poppy Seed Waffle Pancakes

Ingredients:

- 1 cup all-purpose flour
- 1 tbsp sugar
- 1 tsp baking powder
- 1/4 tsp salt
- 1 tbsp poppy seeds
- Zest of 1 lemon
- 3/4 cup milk
- 1 egg
- 2 tbsp melted butter
- 1 tbsp lemon juice
- 1/2 tsp vanilla

Instructions:
Mix dry ingredients. In another bowl, whisk wet ingredients and zest.
Combine and cook in a waffle iron until lightly golden.
Serve with lemon glaze or fresh berries.

Cranberry Orange Waffle Pancakes
Ingredients:

- 1 cup all-purpose flour
- 1 tbsp sugar
- 1 tsp baking powder
- 1/2 tsp salt
- Zest of 1 orange
- 3/4 cup milk
- 1 egg
- 2 tbsp melted butter
- 1/2 tsp vanilla
- 1/2 cup chopped fresh or dried cranberries

Instructions:
Combine dry and wet ingredients separately, then mix together. Fold in cranberries.
Cook in a waffle iron until golden and crispy.
Top with orange marmalade or maple syrup.

Waffle Pancakes with Fresh Mango Salsa

Ingredients:

For the waffle pancakes:

- 1 cup all-purpose flour
- 1 tbsp sugar
- 1 tsp baking powder
- 1/4 tsp salt
- 3/4 cup milk
- 1 egg
- 2 tbsp melted butter
- 1/2 tsp vanilla

For the mango salsa:

- 1 ripe mango (diced)
- 1 tbsp lime juice
- 1 tbsp chopped mint or cilantro
- 1 tsp honey (optional)

Instructions:

Prepare waffle pancake batter and cook in waffle iron.
Toss mango salsa ingredients together.
Serve waffles topped with the fresh salsa for a sweet-tangy twist.

Almond Joy Waffle Pancakes
Ingredients:

- 1 cup all-purpose flour
- 2 tbsp cocoa powder
- 1 tbsp sugar
- 1 tsp baking powder
- 1/4 tsp salt
- 3/4 cup coconut milk
- 1 egg
- 2 tbsp melted butter
- 1/4 cup shredded coconut
- 1/4 cup mini chocolate chips
- 2 tbsp chopped almonds

Instructions:
Mix dry ingredients. Combine wet ingredients, then fold in coconut, chocolate chips, and almonds.
Cook in a waffle iron until crispy.
Serve with chocolate drizzle and more coconut.

Sweet and Salty Waffle Pancakes with Pretzels
Ingredients:

- 1 cup all-purpose flour
- 1 tbsp sugar
- 1 tsp baking powder
- 1/4 tsp salt
- 3/4 cup milk
- 1 egg
- 2 tbsp melted butter
- 1/4 cup crushed pretzels
- Optional: chocolate chips or caramel sauce

Instructions:
Whisk dry and wet ingredients separately, then mix. Fold in crushed pretzels.
Cook in waffle iron.
Top with a mix of crushed pretzels, a drizzle of caramel, or a sprinkle of sea salt.

Mocha Chip Waffle Pancakes
Ingredients:

- 1 cup all-purpose flour
- 2 tbsp sugar
- 1 tbsp cocoa powder
- 1 tsp baking powder
- 1/4 tsp salt
- 3/4 cup milk
- 1/4 cup strong brewed coffee (cooled)
- 1 egg
- 2 tbsp melted butter
- 1/4 cup mini chocolate chips

Instructions:
Combine dry and wet ingredients, then fold in chocolate chips.
Cook in a waffle iron until done.
Serve with espresso whipped cream or chocolate syrup.

Caramel Waffle Pancakes with Pecans

Ingredients:

- 1 cup all-purpose flour
- 1 tbsp brown sugar
- 1 tsp baking powder
- 1/4 tsp salt
- 3/4 cup milk
- 1 egg
- 2 tbsp melted butter
- 1/4 cup chopped pecans
- Caramel sauce (for topping)

Instructions:
Mix dry ingredients. In another bowl, whisk milk, egg, and butter.
Combine and fold in pecans.
Cook in waffle iron until golden and crisp.
Drizzle with warm caramel sauce and top with extra pecans if desired.

Churro Waffle Pancakes

Ingredients:

- 1 cup all-purpose flour
- 2 tbsp sugar
- 1 tsp baking powder
- 1/4 tsp salt
- 3/4 cup milk
- 1 egg
- 2 tbsp melted butter
- 1/2 tsp vanilla
- 1/4 cup cinnamon sugar (for coating)

Instructions:
Make batter and cook waffles.
While warm, brush with melted butter and coat generously in cinnamon sugar.
Serve with chocolate sauce for dipping.

Waffle Pancakes with Peanut Butter and Jelly
Ingredients:

- 1 cup all-purpose flour
- 1 tbsp sugar
- 1 tsp baking powder
- 1/4 tsp salt
- 3/4 cup milk
- 1 egg
- 2 tbsp peanut butter (softened)
- 2 tbsp melted butter
- Grape or strawberry jam (for topping)

Instructions:
Mix dry ingredients. Whisk wet ingredients with peanut butter until smooth.
Combine and cook in waffle iron.
Top with swirls of jelly and more peanut butter if desired.

Cherry Cheesecake Waffle Pancakes
Ingredients:

- 1 cup all-purpose flour
- 1 tbsp sugar
- 1 tsp baking powder
- 1/4 tsp salt
- 3/4 cup milk
- 1 egg
- 2 tbsp melted butter
- 1/2 tsp vanilla
- 1/4 cup cream cheese (softened)
- Cherry pie filling or fresh cherries (for topping)

Instructions:
Prepare batter and cook in waffle iron.
Spread a layer of whipped or softened cream cheese over the waffles.
Top with cherry filling or fresh cherries.

Dark Chocolate Raspberry Waffle Pancakes
Ingredients:

- 1 cup all-purpose flour
- 2 tbsp cocoa powder
- 2 tbsp sugar
- 1 tsp baking powder
- 1/4 tsp salt
- 3/4 cup milk
- 1 egg
- 2 tbsp melted butter
- 1/4 cup dark chocolate chips
- 1/2 cup fresh or frozen raspberries

Instructions:
Mix dry ingredients, then wet. Fold in chocolate chips and raspberries.
Cook until crisp in waffle iron.
Serve with a dusting of powdered sugar or dark chocolate drizzle.

Cinnamon Apple Waffle Pancakes
  Ingredients:

- 1 cup all-purpose flour
- 1 tbsp brown sugar
- 1 tsp baking powder
- 1/2 tsp cinnamon
- 1/4 tsp salt
- 3/4 cup milk
- 1 egg
- 2 tbsp melted butter
- 1/2 cup finely diced apple (peeled)

Instructions:
Whisk dry ingredients. Mix wet ingredients and combine. Fold in apple pieces.
Cook until golden brown.
Serve with maple syrup and a sprinkle of cinnamon sugar.

www.ingramcontent.com/pod-product-compliance
Lightning Source LLC
LaVergne TN
LVHW081325060526
838201LV00055B/2472